Copyright © 2022 by Nailah Harvey of **N.HARV LLC**.
All rights reserved.

You are welcome to print a copy of this workbook for your personal use. Other than that, no part of this publication may be reproduced, stored, or transmitted in any form or by any means, electronic, mechanical, photocopying, recording, scanning, or otherwise, except permitted under Section 107 or 108 of the 1976 United States Copyright Act, without the prior written permission of the author. Requests to the author and publisher for permission should be addressed to nailah@nharv.com.

ISBN: 979-8-218-03356-9

Because of the dynamic nature of the internet, any web addresses or links contained in this book may have changed since publication and may no longer be valid. The views expressed in this work are solely those of the author and do not necessarily reflect the views of the publisher, and the publisher disclaims any responsibility for them.

Website: www.nharv.com

Printed in the United States of America

Book-fluence:

How to Write a Book to Position Yourself as a Leader in Your Industry

Nailah Harvey, M.A.Ed

This book is for the leader who had dreams of becoming an author one day.

Allow me to help make your dreams a reality by teaching you how to leverage your leadership into a strategically written, informational book.

Legal Disclaimer

My advice and strategies are to support you in your author goals, but your success depends on your own effort, commitment, and follow through. Unfortunately, I cannot guarantee your book influence or "bookfluence," but I genuinely hope you achieve success.

Table of Contents

Introduction 11

The Importance of Influence 15

Work on Your Author Mindset 19

Record Your Expertise 25

Identify Your Framework 31

Tailor Your Book 35

Expand Your Influence 39

The Self-Publishing Secrets 47

Introduction

"If only you had a book about how to write a book..."

I had just wrapped up my speech at Compton College about my book-writing process, when one of the attendees walked up and said this to me. As I marinated on her comment, I realized that while I had packaged some of my experiences into books—after all, I'd written my *SoKoDiaries* book series about my time as a Black American living and teaching in South Korea—I didn't have anything published that could provide a solution for aspiring authors. I didn't have the authority by way of a subject-specific book to help people achieve this desired result.

I, a qualified educator, didn't take advantage of the opportunity to meet the needs of the Compton College students. I dropped the ball...in my own hometown. Those scholars needed to see someone whose influential views on book writing were supported by research and theories. They needed proof of concept. They deserved to learn how to structure their ideas and outline their manuscripts. Unfortunately, I did not help them develop this skill set. I inspired the students for an hour, and then left them without a tangible resource to supplement my signature talk. I left them without an opportunity to connect with me in the future. This mistake probably caused me multiple speaking opportunities and thousands of dollars – literally.

That's why we're here.

I want to talk to you about the importance of influence as it pertains to authorship. I want to show you how you can stand out as a leader in your industry by organizing your expertise into a nonfiction book. Afterall, you can't spell the word authority without "author." 😊 What makes you an authority, you ask? Someone who has authority has the power to influence or command thought, opinion, or behavior. What makes you an authority figure in your industry, you ask? You have the knowledge, expertise, and solutions due to your years of experience, trial, and error. Your knowledge and expertise is based on an accumulation of education, research, and life experience. So why not take all that you've accumulated and turn it into a book that will increase your authority?

My goal is to bridge the gap between leadership and influence by teaching you how to become a **bookfluencer**, which is a leader who influences people by way of his or her book. Does an expert have to write a book to be considered an influencer, a leader, or an authority? Of course not. But writing a book gives you recognition as well as the chance to be sought after. A book can be the type of influence that you need to set you apart from your peers and produce opportunity after opportunity for years to come.

Who is "Book-Fluence: How to Write a Book to Position Yourself as a Leader in Your Industry" for?

Book-fluence is for educators and administrators who desire to impact students inside and outside of the classroom.

Book-fluence is for service providers who are tired of physically performing a skill to earn an income.

Book-fluence is for online business owners who are looking for a lead-generator for prospective course and coaching clients.

Book-fluence is for everyday professionals who lead teams, organizations, or ministries... and would like to leverage that leadership by way of a book.

~

There's an audience waiting to hear your approach to the field you've been in for the past five-plus years. Imagine writing something that you can leave with supporters long after your conversation or experience with them ends. I learned my lesson from Compton College years ago. After that speaking engagement, I started improving my book-writing skills, which eventually turned into a reference book (in 2016)—a book that I will probably monetize and market for the rest of my life. *Look Better In Writing:*

A Quick and Easy Guide to Punctuation is a grammar guide that's currently housed on Amazon as well as in a few college libraries. No, it's not a book about the book-writing process per say, but it still solves a general writing problem: grammar. I wrote it in grad school for other grad students (as well as myself) to provide quick grammar tips to minimize time researching proper punctuation while writing term papers. I used all my years of experience as an English teacher to provide a solution for busy college students.

It's important to note that *Look Better In Writing* was not my first book, as I mentioned my *SoKoDiaries* book series early in the chapter. This was my sixth book, yet it was the first informational book that I've ever written. The theme was intentional, but the structure of the book came after years of honing my craft. Since its release date, *Look Better In Writing* has expanded into a podcast, an online community, and soon to be K-12 curriculum. The expertise turned into the book…and the book turned into the business…and beyond. That's bookfluence!

How does this relate to you? Well, if I can do it, you can, too. You've studied and practiced your skill set for years, and *Book-fluence: How to Write a Book to Position Yourself as a Leader in Your Industry* will equip you with a five-part process to leverage your leadership and **w.r.i.t.e.** an impactful, informational book.

The Importance of Influence

Leadership is influencing people toward a purpose. Think of your favorite boss. I'm not saying that everyone with influence is a leader, but I am saying that *good* leadership persuades others to make decisions based on the recommendation of someone who is highly regarded, respected and/or well-known or well-resourced. This is influence as it relates to leadership.

It's a little-known fact that bloggers, magazine editors, and journalists, have the power to shape a story and a narrative that leads people toward a decision. That's not only the power of words, but it's the power of effective communication. It's the power of leadership. *Influence is leadership.* And if writing is a form of leadership, then writing is also a form of influence.

A special shout out to my fellow online business owners—listen to me, you are a leader. The years you've put into building and scaling your business and managing your team has equipped you as such. The years you've put into failing and succeeding has equipped you as such. You're already halfway there to becoming the go-to expert in your industry. Show people that you can not only **do** your work, but you can **teach** your work.

How to Determine Your Influence

What are you great at? Not good. The world has enough people who are "good" at things. I want you to push past mediocrity and think about the things you can do with your eyes closed or the topics you can speak about without any moment's notice. Think about what makes you feel valuable after doing it. Think about what makes you smile while talking about it. What do people come to you for?

Once you've reflected, ask yourself if there's a market need for your skill set or thought leadership. Meaning, are people looking for or buying something similar? Are colleges, companies, conferences, or churches paying people to speak about something similar? Have people validated your expertise? Or is your target audience creating workarounds because the solution or packaging of information does not exist? Do the research. Fill the gap. Hone your craft. Think of others instead of yourself. The power shifts once you focus on your audience.

What Do You Want to be Known For?

What do you want people to say about you when you leave the room? What do you want people to say about your work? Sure, you can be known for inspiring others, but I challenge you to think about your business. People typically don't pay for inspiration. They pay for solutions. That said, what solution do you want to be known for providing? Think about the leads that will come with writing a book. Think about the validation of your knowledge.

I don't want you to think that I'm pigeonholing you, but if someone doesn't know what to tell people about you, your brand is not...polished. I'm not saying you have to stick with one thing, but you should know what your "one thing" is. Write a book about it. This can be your signature book. Let people know what to focus on concerning your personal brand or your business.

What Should You Write Your Book About?

You may be clear on your skill set, but still unclear on how to niche down a book topic. Here's a tip: write about one subject in your industry and approach it from different angles. For example, if you're a hairstylist in the beauty industry, consider writing about one hairstyle (e.g., knotless braids, flat twists, etc.) for a specific demographic (i.e., millennial Black women, Latino teenagers, etc.), and give your method for attaining said hairstyle. You can also share why and how this hairstyle is beneficial to your audience. Writing about one subject allows you to streamline your topic as well as your audience. It allows you to position yourself as an authority in that specific subject matter.

I recommend writing methodologically when it comes to informational books because methods give you permission to educate your readers/audience with steps. And let's be honest, steps help us all consume information easier.

~

Make sure you do a little market research before you write your book. Ask people about their pet peeves pertaining to your field. Use surveys and forums to get information. For example, there's an online search engine called answerthepublic.com that can be used to identify your target audience's needs and unanswered questions. Business owners and service providers, ask former (and prospective) clients and customers what attracted them to your brand. Corporate professionals, ask your colleagues and team members why they like your approach to your "one thing." Educators and administrators, observe how students, faculty, and staff respond when you speak on certain topics.

On the road to authorship, treat every encounter with your audience as an opportunity to course-correct or polish your work, if needed. Knowing what your people need and finding resources to help them meet that need will exemplify your leadership skills and maximize your influence.

LESSON RECAP: *Show people that you can not only* **do** *your work, but you can* **teach** *your work…and do this by way of a book.*

Work on Your Author Mindset

There are many excuses that will keep you from writing your book. While I believe excuses are valid, I also believe we have to call a thing, a thing. We have to learn how to identify our excuses, our flaws, and our fears so we can healthily overcome them. Notice I'm speaking as "we" right now because I want you to know that I'm not above you. Although my first book was written and published almost 10 years ago, I still experience doubt, angst, and other hindrances (excuses) every time I write a new book. But thankfully, I've developed some mental stamina along the way, and I want to tell you that it all starts with the mind.

This first step in working on your author mindset is to NOT think of the book-writing process as writing a book, but think of it as organizing your expertise into a book. *Feel that release of pressure?* Don't think about the table of contents, word count, editing, etc. Start by thinking of your audience and how you can serve them with what comes easily to you.

The second step is to look at your book as a value-add that will yield a return on investment (ROI). Envision a future that looks different than where you are now—a future graced with opportunities resulting from your bold decision to become an author. Don't get distracted by the cost of writing and publishing your book; understand the cost of NOT sharing your gift with the world.

Speaking of cost, here are a few general book expenses to prepare for:

- $10/month Google Docs (if you're not writing the manuscript in Microsoft Word or another word-processing program)
- $15-$150 monthly newsletter software to email your audience about book updates, launch strategies, the release date, and so on
- $100-$500 front and back cover designs
- $900-$3000 professional editor
- $50-150 interior design
- $6,000 book coach

No, every expense is not necessary, but this gives an idea of the investment that a lot of my clients and peers have made. I've also invested thousands into book coaching and honing my craft. And I get it. Things can seem costly upfront, but again, consider the cost of NOT writing your informational book:

- The missed opportunity of a bulk order of books to a college, company, or organization that will use your content to achieve a result
- The missed opportunity of new sales from the book that you turned into a $500-plus online course
- The missed opportunity of a paid speaking gig—centered around your book topic—in front of hundreds of your ideal clients

- The missed opportunity to expand your influence and leave a legacy with your written words

~

Making the time to sit and write a book takes discipline. You may have to set Google reminders to write 30 minutes a day. You may have to block out time on your calendar. I've found that busy professionals are more likely to do things that are added to our calendar. But what happens when you've done all that and you're still twirling your thumbs with a blank document? That's where your author mindset must kick in again. Think of the end result, and work backwards. Start by setting a future book goal. For instance, if your goal is to get a book out immediately, then you can go to Amazon's Kindle Direct Publishing (KDP) platform at https://kdp.amazon.com/en_US/, sign up, and follow the steps to publish your book on Amazon for free. It takes approximately 24 hours for approval. If your goal, however, is to be on Amazon's bestsellers list, then you need to be more strategic with your publishing. You may want to incorporate more social media promotion, more email marketing, and more book launch strategies. You may also want to make your book available for pre-order. This has the potential to get people more excited about your product—which will make your product more popular. After all, "bestseller" is code for "most popular."

What Are Your Book Goals?

You can further define your book goal(s) by asking yourself these questions:

- **What do I want to gain from writing this book?**
- **Who do I want to serve?** (e.g., Baby Boomers in Corporate America, HBCU doctoral students, Gen X ministry leaders, etc.)
- **How far would I like my reach?** (i.e., local, national, global)
- **How will my book solve my readers' problem or transform their life/business?**

~

Leaders, while you're possibly overcoming mental blocks centered around becoming an author, I want to encourage you with an analogy from marketing influencer, Mahdi Woodard about practicing at the top of your license. Think about what happens when you or someone you know visits a medical specialist...let's say an ophthalmologist. A standard check-in typically includes paperwork and a vision assessment. This is all prep work done *before* the doctor comes in. In most cases, the specialist is skilled to complete these tasks, but instead, he or she focuses on what they've spent years of training on: providing patients with eye care services to ensure good eye health. Ophthalmologists are leaders so they practice at the top of their license. Meaning, they provide optimal solutions to their patients by focusing on their best skill set.

Learn from your medical specialist. Be a responsible steward of your talents. Lean into your calling. Practice at the top of your industry, so you pass the wisdom down by way of a book. Concentrate the bulk of your research, time, and energy on a specific subject matter and demographic. Know that you are built for this. Remember, the most important influence is your mind. Lead it, so you can lead others.

LESSON RECAP: *The most important influence is your mind. Lead it, so you can lead others.*

Record Your Expertise

The way you show up daily and contribute your skill set to your job and/or business is admirable, but what happens if you suddenly get called to speak at a major conference and the attendees want more access to your know-how? What if they want your book but you don't have one? And what happens when if receive multiple inquiries about "how you got to where you are" and you don't have the capacity or time to respond to everyone? Don't get caught slippin', leaders. It's time to think and plan ahead. Document your processes, or as I like to say, record your expertise.

You're busy. I get it. But trust me, recording your expertise will allow you to automate your processes, and then delegate (accordingly) to team members—which graces you with time to "practice at the top of your license." *Again, think ahead.* Write things out step by step. This will give space to tighten up your systems, recognize how much work you actually do, and discover tasks that can be assigned to others. Hopefully, after writing things out, you'll feel more confident in not only packaging your expertise but packaging your transformation. The goal is greater impact, less time.

Before you get started with listing out your tasks, keep your book atop of mind...and give it a title. This is the first step in recording your expertise because it's like having a thesis statement for your college paper. You start with the main topic, and then build your ideas around it. When creating a book title, here's a formula that my book coach taught me. Create a title that is the desired solution for your readers and a subtitle that tells them how to achieve the goal. Hence, *Book-fluence: How to Write a Book to Position Yourself as a Leader in Your Industry.* A few other book title examples are:

- *Published & Paid: Self-Publish and Launch Your Nonfiction Book in 90 Days or Less*
- *14 Secrets to a Done Dissertation: A Guide to Navigation to Dissertation Process and Finishing in Record Time*
- *Cracking the Code: The Blueprint for Entrepreneurs to Secure High-Paying Contracts with Schools*

Marketable book titles help you influence people to buy the book without reading through it first. Cue, pre-orders and online orders. Book titles, in general, help the author stay in alignment with his or her message. That's why it's step number one in the "record your expertise" exercise.

What are three possible book titles for your book? (Keep the title seven words or less and the subtitle 15 words or less.)

1. _____

2. _____

3. _____

Now that you've narrowed down your book titles to three possibilities, ask your audience which title resonates best with them. A strategy I share with my coaching clients is to search your possible book titles on Google to (1) see if it's been used, and/or (2) see how many people have researched similar titles or keywords. The more a title (or a variation of it) has been searched, the more people want to know about it. This is a good thing if you're looking to position yourself as a subject matter expert. Now, pick your favorite title, and let's move on to second part of this exercise.

~

Once you've picked your favorite book title, you can officially start recording your expertise. List the tasks that enable you to reach the same solution as your book title. Document your processes and organize them into themes. I challenge you to choose five themes centered around your book title. Even if you list 27 tasks after recording your expertise, find a way to organize them into the five themes. The themes will eventually turn into chapters.

Here's a little trick I like to use when arranging my book chapters—I call it the I.D.I.O.T. process. I'm not calling anyone an idiot; I just like using acronyms because they help information to stick. Anyway, the I.D.I.O.T. process allows you to arrange your book chapters by introduction, definition, identification, opinion, and transformation. Most books start with an introduction, so let's not reinvent the wheel here. **Introduce** yourself, your book, and its purpose. The next chapters will **define** what you'll talk about and **identify** any examples needed to further explain your subject matter. The other chapters are reserved to express your **opinions** (if any), and the final chapter will **transform** all the inclusive themes into a conclusion.

Think of five possible themes that can double as chapter titles. Arrange them according to the I.D.I.O.T. process. If you need more chapters to get your point across, feel free to add them accordingly.

1. _____
2. _____
3. _____
4. _____
5. _____

Once you've written out your chapter titles, it's time to write your book! By now, the book-writing process should feel a little less overwhelming because you have an outline. Simply flesh out the ideas in each chapter. Turn your tasks into full sentences and paragraphs, explaining the *what*, *why*, and *how* of your book title.

Before you know it, you'll have the first draft of your manuscript completed. I feel like I need to end with this: DO NOT WRITE AND EDIT AT THE SAME TIME!

LESSON RECAP: *Recording your expertise will allow you to automate your processes, and then delegate (accordingly) to team members—which graces you with time to "practice at the top of your license."*

Identify Your Framework

While recording your expertise, you will have likely noticed a list of repeatable steps to complete the overall goal of your book title. This is your main process, which can turn into your framework. Think of a framework as a teacher's instructional lesson plan—a means to accomplish a teacher's goal and the learning objectives for his or her students. Well, in your business or career, view your framework as a means to walk your clients and colleagues through a step-by-step process to achieve a goal or solve a problem. Once you've documented the ways you personally use your skills to reach a goal, it's time to share the process to help transform someone else's life, career, or business.

How to Create a Framework

There are various ways to create a framework, but let's keep it simple and revisit the exercise from the previous chapter. Look at your original list of tasks (before you broke it down into themes/chapters) and condense your processes into 3-7 steps. Combine tasks if you have to. From the shorter list, try to create an acronym with the first letter of each step. For example, a nurse writing a book about how to successfully draw blood might have a framework like:

- **S**et temperature to cool for a relaxing environment
- **E**ngage with each patient

- Test out veins in both arms to see which is best

In this framework example, the nurse shared an easy way to explain her normal day-to-day tasks. (Her tasks were condensed into three steps). And the people who will read her book and desire to learn this skill set will see this framing of tasks as doable. With regards to your book, if you can't create a sensible acronym with your list, then don't force it. However, you should still break down your tasks into 3-7 memorable steps. It's a win-win for both the reader and the author.

PAUSE: Take a time-out from reading, go back to the Table of Contents in this book, and check out my framework: **w.r.i.t.e**.:

W=ork on your author mindset
R=ecord your expertise
I=dentify your framework
T=ailor your book
E=xpand your influence

I'm not advising that you include your framework in your Table of Contents like I did. I just wanted you to see that I practice what I preach. *wink, wink*

~

Writing an informational book allows you to go from helping one person at a time to many at a time. It increases your reach and therefore expands your influence. What's the hack? Including repeatable, reusable, and proven steps in your book. This ensures that your book (and framework) is timeless. Creating an evergreen resource is a scalable business tactic. If your information is relevant, then you're relevant. And just like it takes more than an effective lesson plan for a teacher's overall success, your framework is only part of the overall success of your book. Nevertheless, don't ignore it because it's what will set your book apart from your peers.

LESSON RECAP: *Include repeatable, reusable, and proven steps in your book. This ensures that your book (and framework) is timeless. Creating an evergreen resource is a scalable business tactic.*

Tailor Your Book

After you write the first draft of your manuscript, go back and remove the unnecessary, and then tailor your book to match your unique voice. FYI, I'm going to say the phrase "tailor-make" in this chapter, but please do not repeat this because it is not 100% grammatically correct. Ha!

Before we get into tailor-making your book, let's talk about removing the unnecessary. I struggle with this book-writing step because I feel like everything I write is necessary. All words matter! Everything I've researched is necessary because I took the time to make it happen. But that's me being lofty and unwise about my audience. Everything originally written in your manuscript is NOT for your readers' eyes. This is a dual-purposed tip as your fellow bookfluencer and a professional editor.

Delete the content within your book that you feel will confuse your readers. I don't care if it's a statistic that will prove you know what you're talking about. If it's distracting, get rid of it. While writing an informational book, you're going to research a lot. And most times, that research is just for you, the authority. It's to develop your thought leadership in your niche.

Tips for removing the unnecessary a.k.a. self-editing:

- Be mindful of adding lots of quotes, links, footnotes, and references to your book. You

don't want it to become a research paper. Unless that's your goal.
- Edit with your "one thing" in mind. If it sounds like the content is veering away from your subject matter, ditch it.
- Know that what you remove from one book may give you an idea of what to write for another book. 😊

How to Tailor-Make Your Book

Tailor-making your book is making it your own. And you can do this by adding more of your voice. If you have a popular saying or catch phrase, throw it in the mix. You can also include a few contractions if you want to. Write "don't" instead of "do not" if you want to make your work less formal. Include more comedy if that's your tone. Include pictures and graphics if you want more of a visual appeal.

Make your book YOUR book—the book that you're happy to attach your name to. But remember, even though you're tailoring your book to match your voice and style, the reality is, your book is not really for you. **I know. Hypocritical.** Your informational book will always be for your target audience a.k.a. your ideal reader. Sure, you want to be true to yourself and your brand, but the purpose is to position yourself as a leader in your industry. The "positioning" involves serving.

Tailor-make your book by asking yourself these two questions:

1. **Is my book consistent with my brand or the way I want to be perceived?**
2. **Is my book consistent with my target audience persona or the demographics (and psychographics) of my ideal reader?**

When trying to think of an example of a brand that most people recognize, Beyoncé comes to mind. Mrs. Knowles-Carter has the influencer marketing game on lock, in my opinion. I'm not the biggest fan of the popstar's recent music because I'm no longer part of her target audience; however, I appreciate Bey's attention to detail when it comes to tailoring her work. Her influence is undeniable! When you see her Instagram feed, the photos are flawless and tell a story without any words. She knows that's what people expect from her. Bey's "one thing" is flawless-ness, and she never disappoints her audience. I would argue that as confident as Beyonce is in her brand, her work is still audience driven. It's **by** her, but it's **for** her people: the Beehive. And that's not a bad thing…that's smart.

Leaders, that's what I want you to do this with your book. Tailor-make it so that it is **by** you, but **for** your readers. Tug at your audience's heartstrings and get to their pain points. Meet the needs of those who are struggling with something you're very familiar with, but do it authentically.

LESSON RECAP: *Make your book YOUR book—the book that you're happy to attach your name to.*

Expand Your Influence

Expansion is something formed by the broadening or development of something else. A book. One can say that it's an expansion of a skill set or service or lesson plan or speech. Expansion doesn't necessarily focus on amounts, nevertheless, there's a visible result in size difference. Relating this to an influencer, while they may be determined by their follower count, they're judged by their ability to lead someone to visible action. Meaning, the true mark of an influencer is contingent upon his or her leadership abilities.

Think Beyond the Book

Throughout *Book-fluence*, I intentionally refer to the benefits of writing a book as an increase or expansion of influence not just the building of a brand. Is it because one is better than the other? No. A strategically written book can yield both results. I mainly refer to influence because it's broader and is used beyond an online platform—which it is most often associated with. The term influence, as opposed to the term brand, is not directly tied to your story but your skills instead.

So how can you use your book to lead others to take action? There are many ways, but I will focus on what I like to call **the core four**: *a digital course, a coaching program, a continuity offer,* and *a signature talk.* For instance, there are a plethora of books that teach nonfiction book writing as a way to build businesses, but I don't know of one that has content centered around the **w.r.i.t.e.** framework. Why? Because it's uniquely mine. I made it up. Your framework, hopefully, will also be uniquely yours. It, too, will be the heart of your book, which can translate into the modules in your **digital course**, the curriculum in your **coaching program**, the driving factor in your **continuity offer**, and the talking points in your **signature talk**.

~

Ways to influence with a book depend on your industry and skill set. (This is a full-circle moment from the Introduction chapter). Examples:

- If you're a consultant, then you can create a supplemental workbook for the service you provide your clients.
- If you're an academic advisor, you can write a book about how to prevent burnout during enrollment season.
- If you're a doctoral student, you can make good use of the time and energy it took to devote to a period of intensive concentrated learning and write a book about your dissertation topic. You can turn your research into a book.

The Business of Books

As I mentioned in the earlier chapters, think about your future when making book-related decisions and investments. Purchase an International Standard Book Number (ISBN)—which is like a social security number for your book—so you can list your business name as the publisher. People may perceive you a little differently if you have this listed instead of the publishing platform's default name. Let's say your business entity is an LLC and it happens to be the same business name you use for your speaking engagements and other business endeavors. Well, the consistency in naming will feed into your overall branding. This is not a bad thing to consider when thinking about authorship. Don't just publish books, build a book business.

I'm not sure if this is a good place to talk about social media, but let's dive in for a sec. Whether you like it or not, social media is here to stay. It's one of the best ways to market your business. And because you'll be in the "book business" after publishing your book, it's wise to know how to properly use social media as a bookfluencer. Before I give social media tips, let me give the ultimate tip when positioning yourself as a leader in your industry: show up. I heard a marketing influencer tell her audience to show up with the right dress code. Meaning, don't just talk about random things or give information, but present the information in a way that's acceptable to the online platform that you're using. For example, write threads or retweet think pieces about your subject matter on Twitter; create info-based reels on Instagram; write and share articles on LinkedIn; engage in niche-specific groups on Facebook.

Whichever platform you choose, show up correctly for your audience.

That said, don't just let your gems stay on social media because you don't own any of the platforms. You don't control the algorithms, and the lifespan of the posts only lasts minutes, if not seconds. If you're like me, you're not spending an hour and a half creating a gem-dropping IG graphic only for someone to scroll past it because their attention is divided. Nah! I'd rather drop all my gems in a book and keep you locked in on my content for more than a few minutes.

Expand Your Influence by Expanding Your Network

When you collaborate with another expert, you're leveraging their audience. Leverage is created by your network. Another benefit of collaborating with experts, specifically experts within your industry, is that you can refer one another instead of learning a new skill set. Let me break this down. Let's say you're a mortgage broker and a potential home buyer asks you about a specific property in a specific neighborhood. Well, instead of taking time away from mortgage negotiations, you can refer the home buyer to a real estate agent who has sold properties in said neighborhood. This allows both the mortgage broker and real estate agent to operate in their zone of genius like author Gay Hendricks discussed in his book, *The Big Leap*.

This is a rhetorical question, but do you know five leading people in your industry right now? Service providers, what if a prospective client inquired about your services, but it was not an ideal match. Is your network strong enough to refer them to another trusted provider in your field? If 'no' is the answer to these questions, then it's time to expand your network. People like convenience. If you can be a human Google search engine in your industry, then kudos. This positions you to be an even greater leader as it shows that you know the leading players, the competitors, and the who's-who in your space. It shows that you'll go above and beyond the call of duty to serve others.

~

I didn't mention this in chapter four, but before you record your expertise, gather other expert opinions about your book topic. (This can also be a way to expand your network.) Sure, you may be in the field doing the job every day, but there will always be things to learn. Develop your knowledge. There may be facts, processes, and statistics you hadn't heard of, and vice versa. Sharing will not make you look like you don't know what you're talking about. If anything, it will show that you care enough about your audience to seek out advice from other specialists. It will show that you're a leader who believes in community.

Be a good steward of people's trust. Lead them to the best result(s). Point them in the direction of the most aligned expert even when it's not you. But wouldn't it be awesome if you can point your target audience to your book at any time of day?!

~

Why am I not encouraging bookfluencers to just write your story? Because there's a more strategic way to write an influential book. Besides, you don't want to solely empower people; you want to help transform their mindset and lifestyle, which has more impact.

Become one with your skills and thought leadership. You are not just a person with knowledge, you're a person with know-how. There's a difference. You've researched, studied, practiced, and invested in your expertise—which came with sweat equity and other sacrifices over the years. That's not to be taken lightly. So, a moment of silence for the old you: the *you* that would downplay his or her knowledge. It's time to play big.

~

I hope my five-step book-writing process is simple enough for you to **w.r.i.t.e.** your informational book immediately. Sometimes we need a little push until we're confident enough to do things on our own, and I'm here to gently nudge you in the direction of your leadership. To my leaders who desire one-on-one support, you can apply to my "Book to Influence" coaching program at www.nharv.com/bookcoaching. If I can't personally help you write your signature book in 90 days, then I will try my best to put you in the hands of a book coach who can. 😊

Cheers to showing up for yourself and the generation of people coming behind you!

Your fave bookfluencer,

Nailah

The Self-Publishing Secrets

Publishing is just sharing. Many people think that the only way to "share" their book is to publish it on Amazon, and that's not true. Sure, Amazon gives you reach, but I want you to consider other publishing platforms so that you can make a choice that is aligned with your book goals. This is a holistic process.

Speaking of, here's a checklist of what's needed before you self-publish a book on Amazon using their publishing platform. *Shhh!*

✓ **Amazon KDP account** = You must sign up to upload and publish their final manuscript to the platform. The dashboard, otherwise known as the "Bookshelf," is where you input your book title, keywords, categories, etc. These are the details that help readers find your book on Amazon.

✓ **Edited manuscript** = Note that there are four different types of book editing, so choose accordingly. Depending on your need, the editing process may be lengthy because you may need multiple editors. And that's okay! I've listed the four different types of book editing below:

DEVELOPMENTAL EDITING

Developmental editing is an in-depth edit of a manuscript. It focuses on the story's setting, plot, characters, and flow. This editing type is very involved and checks for the fluidity/clarity of the author's content, tone of voice, etc. Developmental editing also examines whether a story is missing something or in need of a few cuts. (Rewrites happen in this editing phase.) Authors, have thick skin when dealing with your developmental editor. They're there to help you develop your story and make it... worth reading.

LINE EDITING

Line editing is a line-by-line review of a writer's manuscript, and it focuses on the structure of the work (i.e., word choices, paragraph usage, etc.). This type of editing doesn't necessarily focus on the story or grammar, but on the "craft" of a manuscript (via @vivien.l.reis). In other words, line editing examines how well a writer can organize his or her words.

COPY EDITING

Copy editing deals with the rules. This is where editors check for grammar, syntax, spelling, sentence structure, and inconsistencies!

PROOFREADING

Proofreading is the absolute last step in the editing process. I REPEAT, proofreading is the absolute last step in the editing process. It's similar to copy editing in the sense that it focuses on the writing rules, but it's more of a review of the overall editing process.

*Try to send your final manuscript to the copy editor at least two months before the release date. This gives the editor time to do their job and complete two to three rounds of edits depending on their pricing package. You also need time to review edits and make changes, if necessary. If your book is more than 20,000 words, shoot for a minimum of three months before the release date.

✓ **Interior formatting a.k.a. Typesetting** = You can't just upload a Microsoft Word doc to Amazon KDP and think it's automatically going to be formatted for a 6x9 book when it's printed. It won't work. My advice is to hire a freelancer to transform your doc into a .MOBI or ePUB file. They will also make sure the file is conducive to your book's trim size. Formatting for a 6x9 book is different from a 5x8 book. *NOTE: Amazon KDP is very particular about interior formatting. If you don't meet their requirements, you will not be able to move past this stage and publish your book on their platform.*

✓ **Professionally designed book cover (front and back)** = When publishing an eBook, the size of the front cover depends on your book's trim size. Things, however, get a little tricky when publishing a paperback because you must also consider the back cover and spine size. You'll need the exact page count from your final (formatted) manuscript so that your designer can calculate the spine width of your paperback cover. This ensures that your book will close properly. *Here's a tip:* ask your designer to give you the front cover first so that *you can promote your book while you wait on the final book cover with the back and spine included.*

✓ **Book description** = This summary is typically between 150-200 words, and it focuses on the reader and what they'll get out of your book. The description is also typically needed for the back covers of paperbacks or hardcovers.

✓ **ISBN** = It's the number that makes your book identifiable on publishing platforms. It's what's needed to get your book into bookstores. ISBNs cost around $125 each. Most self-publishing platforms offer a free option that is platform specific. For example, Amazon KDP offers a free 10-digit Amazon Standard Identification Number (ASIN). There are pros and cons to not purchasing an ISBN, but for the sake of this book, which is predicated on influence, I'm going to recommend that you buy one.

✓ **Review digital book proof OR order paperback proof copy** = The digital copy can be reviewed immediately on the publishing platform during the uploading process, but the shipping time for ordering physical proofs depends on your shipping options.

~

Below is a list of two other online publishing platforms I recommend for self-publishing:

- Draft2Digital www.draft2digital.com: This publishing platform distributes eBooks to a variety of retailers including Apple iBooks, Kobo, Barnes & Noble, etc.

- IngramSpark www.ingramspark.com: This publishing platform distributes eBooks, paperbacks, and hardcovers to 40,000+ retailers including Apple iBooks, Barnes & Noble, Walmart.com, Target.com, etc.

If you want to publish your eBook solely on your website, then you don't need to worry about interior formatting/typesetting or purchasing an ISBN.

~

Publishing a quality book is worth the investment of time and money. Your future course, coaching program, continuity offer, and signature talk depends on it. Leaders, your book is an extra dose of credibility, so I hope you **w.r.i.t.e.** and publish it with the mindset of a bookfluencer.

References

I want to reference a few websites and articles that served as great resources in my research for this book:

- www.writersdigest.com
- www.ingramspark.com
- https://kdp.amazon.com/en_US/
- www.draft2digital.com
- www.dictionary.com

www.ingramcontent.com/pod-product-compliance
Lightning Source LLC
LaVergne TN
LVHW022001060526
838201LV00048B/1652